# Gray Wolves

By Lisa M. Herrington

D1212421

Nature's CHILDREN™

Children's Press®

An Imprint of Scholastic Inc.

Content Consultants
Ashley Wright
Head Keeper, North America and Polar Frontier
Columbus Zoo and Aquarium

Nikki Smith
Assistant Curator, North America and Polar Frontier
Columbus Zoo and Aquarium

Library of Congress Cataloging-in-Publication Data

Names: Herrington, Lisa M., author.
Title: Gray wolves/by Lisa M. Herrington.
Other titles: Nature's children (New York, N.Y.)
Description: New York, NY: Children's Press, an imprint of Scholastic Inc.,
2018. | Series: Nature's children | Includes bibliographical references and index.
Identifiers: LCCN 2017058822| ISBN 9780531192641 (library binding) |
ISBN 9780531137574 (pbk.)
Subjects: LCSH: Gray wolf—Juvenile literature. | Wolves—Juvenile literature.
Classification: LCC QL737.C22 H468 2018 | DDC 599.773—dc23
LC record available at https://lccn.loc.gov/2017058822

Design by Anna Tunick Tabachnik

Creative Direction: Judith E. Christ for Scholastic

Produced by Spooky Cheetah Press

No part of this publication may be reproduced in whole or in part, or stored in a retrieval system,
or transmitted in any form or by any means, electronic, mechanical, photocopying, recording, or otherwise,
without written permission of the publisher. For information regarding permission, write to Scholastic Inc.,
Attention: Permissions Department, Scholastic Inc., 557 Broadway, New York, NY 10012.
© 2019 Scholastic Inc.

All rights reserved. Published in 2019 by Children's Press, an imprint of Scholastic Inc.

Printed in North Mankato, MN, USA 113

SCHOLASTIC, CHILDREN'S PRESS, NATURE'S CHILDREN™, and associated logos
are trademarks and/or registered trademarks of Scholastic Inc.

1 2 3 4 5 6 7 8 9 10 R 28 27 26 25 24 23 22 21 20 19

Scholastic Inc., 557 Broadway, New York, NY 10012.

Photographs ©: cover: Art Wolfe/Getty Images; 1: imageBROKER/Alamy Images; 4 leaf silo and throughout:
stockgraphicdesigns.com; 4 top: Jim McMahon/Mapman ®); 5 child silo: All-Silhouettes.com; 5 wolf silo: Ksanawo/Shutterstock;
5 bottom: Matthias Breiter/Minden Pictures; 6 wolf silo and throughout: Vectorig/iStockphoto; 7: Paul Sawer/Minden Pictures;
8: Jim Brandenburg/Minden Pictures; 11: Juan Carlos Muñoz/age fotostock; 13: Louise Murray/Visuals Unlimited, Inc./Getty
Images; 15: Ronan Donovan/Getty Images; 16: Paul Sawer/Minden Pictures; 19: Tim Davis/Corbis/VCG/Getty Images; 20:
mlharing/Getty Images; 23 top left: Doug Lindstrand/age fotostock; 23 top right: Mark Raycroft/Minden Pictures; 23 bottom
left: impr2003/iStockphoto; 23 bottom right: traveler1116/iStockphoto; 25: Jim Brandenburg/Minden Pictures; 26: Konrad
Wothe/Minden Pictures; 29: Klein and Hubert/Minden Pictures; 30: Frank Lukasseck/Getty Images; 33: Sue Ruth/New Mexico
Museum of Natural History/Flickr; 34: SashaFoxWalters/iStockphoto; 37: Jim Cumming/Getty Images; 38: Donald M. Jones/age
fotostock; 41: Guy Edwardes/Getty Images; 42 left: Design Pics Inc/Alamy Images; 42 right: ChrisVanLennepPhoto/iStockphoto;
43 top left: KenCanning/iStockphoto; 43 bottom: Jagodka/Shutterstock; 43 top right: Juan Carlos Muñoz/age fotostock.

# Table of Contents

# Fact File: Gray Wolves

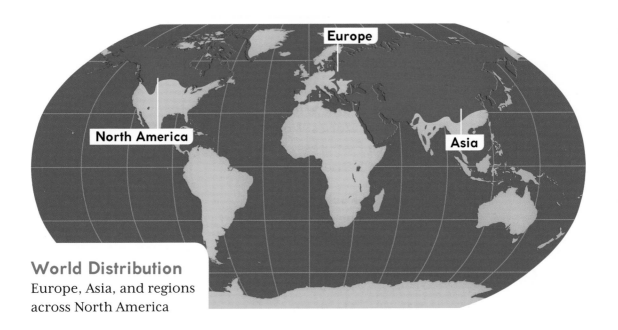

**Europe**

**North America**

**Asia**

## World Distribution
Europe, Asia, and regions across North America

## Habitat
A variety of environments, including forests, mountains, and tundra

## Habits
Intelligent, social, and highly territorial; live, hunt, and raise young in family units; communicate through body language, scent, and howls and other sounds

## Diet
Large animals, such as elk, deer, moose, and caribou; smaller animals such as rabbits, beavers, and mice

## Distinctive Features
Muscular bodies covered in fur; bushy tails; powerful jaws; long legs for distance running

**Fast Fact**
Gray wolves are the largest wild dogs in the world.

## Average Size

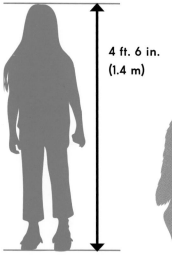

4 ft. 6 in.
(1.4 m)

2 ft. 6 in.
(0.8 m)

Human (age 10)

Gray Wolf (adult)

## Classification

**CLASS**
Mammalia
(mammals)

**ORDER**
Carnivora
(carnivores)

**FAMILY**
Canidae
(dogs, coyotes, foxes,
jackals, and wolves)

**GENUS**
*Canis*
(dogs)

**SPECIES**
*Canis lupus*
(gray wolf)

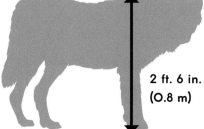

◀ Most gray wolves
are gray or brown.
But their fur can also
be white or even black.

# CHAPTER 1

# Wolves in the Wild

It's quiet in the forest. A chill fills the air. The leaves rustle as something moves through the trees at a brisk trot. From deep in the woods, a creature emerges onto a clearing. It is a gray wolf in search of its family. Stretching its head upward, the wolf howls to call them. The spine-tingling call carries through the air.

Several miles away, a chorus of eerie howls rings out in response. Soon, the wolf reunites with its family, called a **pack**. The wolves are hungry and ready to hunt.

Gray wolves are best known as fierce hunters, so they are often misunderstood. Some people see them only as ferocious killing machines—the bad guys in fairy tales. But these powerful **predators** are some of the most fascinating animals on Earth. Gray wolves are smart and social. They live in close-knit families. And wolves can even be affectionate and playful with each other.

▶ Each gray wolf has a unique howl.

# Where Wolves Wander

Gray wolves live in many **habitats**, including forests, mountains, and cold **tundra**. They need to live in areas that offer plenty of **prey** and water. It also helps to have trees and bushes for cover when possible. Wolves roam far to find food, so they also need a lot of space to hunt.

Most gray wolves live in the northern wilderness, so they have to be able to survive cold temperatures. A wolf's coat is made up of two layers. The outer layer has long, stiff guard hairs that shed water. Underneath is a short layer of thick, soft fur for warmth. The wolf's paws act as snowshoes that keep the wolf from sinking in snow.

Gray wolves were once common across North America, but they were hunted almost to **extinction**. Today, these wolves live in Alaska and Canada and near the western Great Lakes. Some are found in the northern Rocky Mountains and Pacific Northwest. A small population lives in the southwestern United States in Arizona and New Mexico.

◀ Wolves in cold areas often have white fur, which helps them blend in with the snow.

# Fierce Features

Gray wolves have muscular bodies, thick coats, and bushy tails. From their noses to the tips of their tails, these wolves can grow more than 6 feet (1.8 meters) long. That's about as long as your bed! They stand 2 to 3 ft. (0.6 to 0.9 m) tall at the shoulder. Wolves weigh between 70 and 130 pounds (31.8 and 59 kilograms). Males are typically larger than females.

Gray wolves are meat-eaters. They are perfecly built for their hunting lifestyle.

A wolf has 42 sharp teeth—10 more than people—which include four bladelike canine teeth that are used to grab prey. Their powerful jaws can crush a moose's bones.

The wolves' long legs help them run far and chase down food. Huge paws and claws help them move through and over rough ground. When they want to move faster, wolves run on their toes.

**Fast Fact**
A wolf's paw is about the size of an adult human's hand.

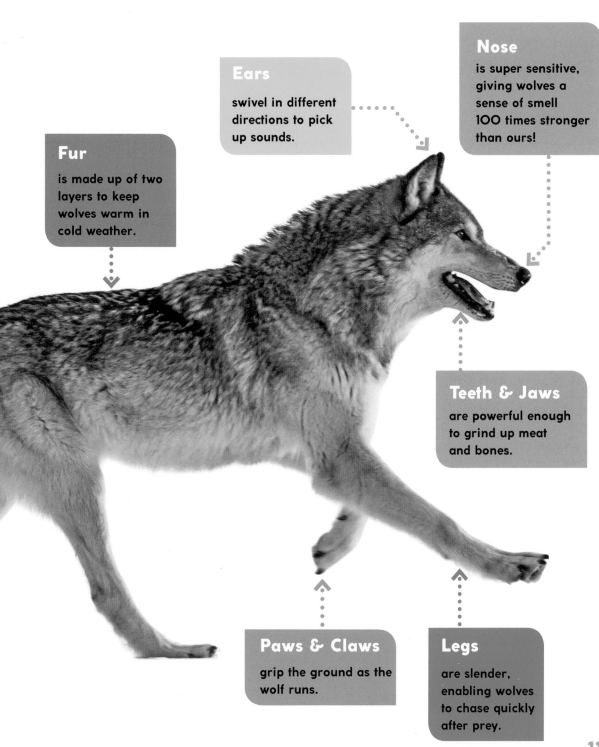

**Ears**

swivel in different directions to pick up sounds.

**Nose**

is super sensitive, giving wolves a sense of smell 100 times stronger than ours!

**Fur**

is made up of two layers to keep wolves warm in cold weather.

**Teeth & Jaws**

are powerful enough to grind up meat and bones.

**Paws & Claws**

grip the ground as the wolf runs.

**Legs**

are slender, enabling wolves to chase quickly after prey.

11

# Sharp Senses

When a dog sniffs the ground, it is gathering information about its surroundings. Wolves do the same thing. These animals rely on their strong senses of smell, sound, and sight to hunt and survive.

Wolves can smell an animal before they see it. They can sniff out a moose more than 1 mile (1.6 km) away and then track it down. They're able to do this thanks to the more than 200 million scent cells inside their noses.

Wolves also hear 20 times better than we do. They use their exceptional hearing to detect even the quietest prey moving in the woods.

Wolves see better at night than people, too. Their eyes have a special light-reflecting layer that makes them glow in the dark. Scientists think this might help them pick up details and spot movement in the dark.

▶ Wolves use their noses to pick up different scents.

# CHAPTER 2

# Life in a Pack

Gray wolves are social animals. Most live in families called packs. A pack can include anywhere from two to 30 wolves. But most are made up of six to eight members. Pack members protect and take care of each other. They hunt, eat, and sleep together.

Each pack has its own **territory** where it lives and hunts. The territory's size mainly depends on how much food is available. It may range from 50 square miles (129.5 square kilometers) to 1,000 sq. mi. (2,590 sq km). If food is plentiful, the territory is small. If wolves need more space to hunt, the territory is larger.

Wolves use scent to communicate. They mark the borders of their territory by spraying urine on trees and rocks. Some wolves scratch the ground, using scent **glands** between their claws to spread their smell. The smell warns other packs to stay away. Wolves defend their territory and will ferociously fight an invading pack.

▶ **A wolf pack works as a team to guard its land.**

# Follow the Leaders

A wolf pack is made up of different family members. Two parents lead the pack. They are sometimes called the alpha male and alpha female. The pack includes the alphas' children. It can also include aunts, uncles, and unrelated wolves.

Each wolf has its own **rank** above or below other wolves in the pack. The parents are the **dominant** wolves. They guide the pack and set the rules. They decide when the pack will hunt, and they often eat first.

Pack members communicate through body language. Wolves rub or lick each other to show affection. They show anger by baring their teeth. Rank is also communicated through body language. A dominant wolf holds its tail and ears high. A lower-ranking wolf makes itself look smaller when approaching the dominant animal. It may crouch down, hold its tail between its legs, or roll over.

◀ A high-ranking wolf uses body language to show that it's the boss.

# Howls and Growls

Wolves make different sounds to "talk" to each other, but they are most famous for their howls. A wolf's howl is a call to other wolves. When a wolf starts howling, others in the pack usually join in. Their howls can make the pack seem bigger than it is.

Scientists think wolves howl for different reasons. A wolf howls to find its pack if it has become separated, or to call members of the pack together. Sometimes, wolves howl to warn other wolves to stay out of their territory.

Many people think that wolves howl *at* full moons. But they're really just pointing their heads toward the sky so their calls travel farther. Wolves actually howl both during the day and at night—whether there's a full moon or not.

Wolves make other noises, too. A wolf will growl or snarl when it feels angry or threatened. Wolves may whine and whimper when they are excited, frustrated, being friendly, or showing affection.

▶ The pack's howls can be heard up to 10 miles (16.1 km) away.

# Hungry Hunters

Life isn't easy for gray wolves. Imagine walking eight hours a day just to find food! It's normal for these predators to spend most of their time looking for their dinner.

Wolves have great speed and **endurance**. They travel huge distances—up to 30 mi. (48.3 km) a day—while hunting. The wolves usually trot along at about 5 miles per hour (8 kilometers per hour). But when pursuing prey, they can sprint up to 40 mph (64.4 km/h).

But most hunts are not successful. Wolves may eat one to three times a week. However, sometimes it takes them up to two weeks to find food. When they catch food, they really do "wolf" it down. A wolf can devour 20 lb. (9.1 kg) of food in one meal. That would be like you eating 100 hamburgers for dinner!

◀ Wolves feast on a meal as ravens flock nearby. These birds often follow wolves and dine on their leftovers.

# What's for Dinner?

Wolf packs usually eat large animals with hooves, including moose, deer, elk, bison, and caribou. They also hunt smaller animals like rabbits, beavers, and mice. Wolves sometimes kill farm animals like cows and sheep, and they will even snack on plants and fruit.

It would be difficult for a single wolf to take down a large animal. A moose might weigh 10 times as much as a wolf. So a pack works as a team.

A pack may trail an animal for miles by following its scent. As the wolves creep closer, they stay hidden. Then they bolt at lightning speed. Usually one wolf lunges at the prey and grabs hold with its jaws. Then the others attack.

If the prey is part of a herd, the pack will try to separate that animal from the rest of the group and circle it. Then they go in for the kill. They often attack sick or injured animals because they are easier to catch. This helps keep herds healthy since wolves take out the weakest animals.

▶ Wolves hunt many different kinds of animals.

**Moose**

Moose may fight back or simply stand and stare at the wolves until they give up.

**Deer**

▶ Many deer are fast enough to outrun gray wolves.

**Snowshoe Hare**

▶ Wolves eat these rabbits that live in cold areas.

**Elk**

Teamwork helps wolves take down these huge animals.

# Bringing Up Pups

Packs also raise babies, called pups, as a family, too. The dominant male and female are the only members of the pack that **mate**. Wolves are very loyal and typically stay together for life. Mating usually takes place between January and March.

The mother is pregnant for about 63 days. In the spring, she gives birth to a **litter** of four to six pups. The pups are born in a warm, cozy **den**. A wolf may dig a hole for its den or use a hollow log.

Newborn pups are helpless. They cannot hear or see. Their eyes are shut, and they have little fur. They weigh only 1 lb. (0.5 kg) and are about as big as an adult's hand.

At first, the babies snuggle and keep warm against their mother. Like people, wolves are **mammals**. Females make milk for their babies. The pups **nurse** for a month or so. During that time, the mother rarely leaves the den. The father and other wolves bring her food.

▶ **A mother wolf cuddles with her litter of pups.**

**Fast Fact**
Most pups are born with blue eyes that later change to gold.

# All in the Family

Wolves grow quickly. By two to three weeks old, the pups have opened their eyes and tripled in weight. They begin to hear, stand, and walk. They squeak, whine, and grunt.

After about four weeks, their fuzzy coats start to change to adult fur. The babies leave the den for the first time. They venture outside to play and explore. The entire pack starts to care for the pups. They protect them from eagles, bears, and other dangers. One of the adults will babysit the pups if the mother goes hunting with the pack.

When adult wolves return from hunting, the pups are hungry. They lick at the adults' mouths to ask for food. Grown wolves **regurgitate**, or spit up, their swallowed meat to feed the pups.

At 8 to 10 weeks old, the pups start eating solid meat. While the adults hunt, the pups wait in new areas away from the den called rendezvous sites.

◀ Pups lick an adult wolf's mouth when they want to be fed.

# Tag, You're It!

Gray wolf pups are a lot like you! They learn as they grow, just as you do. The pups like to play tag and hide-and-seek. They are practicing important skills and preparing to become strong hunters.

The pups playfully wrestle and tumble with their brothers and sisters. They romp and roll in the grass. They climb on adults. They nip at one another's ears and tails. They stalk and chase each other. They pounce on mice. They use bones and sticks as chew toys.

All this play teaches young wolves many lessons. They learn how to communicate. They establish pack behavior and form close **bonds**. Wolves learn how to defend themselves. Later in life, they will use these skills to keep invaders out of their territory. One of these young wolves may one day become a leader of a new pack.

▶ **Pups spend a lot of time playing.**

**Fast Fact**
Wolves sleep in groups. In a storm, they may curl up together.

# Wild Life

By fall, the pups are about six months old. They are almost the size of adult wolves. They will join the pack to search for food. Wolves hunt during the day and night but usually at dusk or dawn. Their prey is most active then.

The following spring, the year-old wolves are fully grown. They help their mother care for a new litter. When the wolf reaches two or three years old, it may stay with its pack and continue to help raise the young, or it may leave and find a mate to begin a new pack. After it leaves the pack, the wolf often lives alone.

Gray wolves usually live six to eight years in the wild. Some die from disease, lack of food, or old age. Others may be killed by humans, other wolves, or even a moose's hoof or an elk's antlers. Wolves living in the care of humans can live up to 20 years.

◀ Gray wolves grow up to be good swimmers. They may even follow prey into water.

# CHAPTER 4

# Blast to the Past

Wolves have roamed Earth for a very long time. Early wolf **ancestors** lived in Asia about 40 million years ago. Over time, these creatures developed into today's wolves.

Scientists think gray wolves **migrated** from Asia to North America about 750,000 years ago. Long ago, a land bridge connected the two continents.

Gray wolves once lived alongside many ancient creatures. These included saber-toothed cats and the gray wolf's cousin, the massive dire wolf. Scientists have discovered that these predators roamed from South America all the way up to Canada. They were more muscular and bigger than today's wolves. They also had stronger bites.

Dire wolves vanished about 10,000 years ago. What caused their disappearance? Humans may have hunted them or hunted the animals they depended on for food.

▶ **This dire wolf skeleton is on display in a museum in New Mexico.**

**Fast Fact**

A wolf's jaw is twice as powerful as that of a German shepherd.

# Canine Cousins

There are two main **species** of wolves: gray wolves and red wolves. In North America, there are five **subspecies** of gray wolves. They are the Canadian/Rocky Mountain, Mexican, Arctic, Great Plains, and Algonquin gray wolves. Some scientists consider Algonquin gray wolves its own separate species.

Red wolves live in a small area of the southeastern United States. They are generally smaller than gray wolves. Very few are left in the wild.

Wolves are cousins of dogs. In fact, scientists think our pet dogs descended from wolves. Dog and wolves are both canines. Wolves look a lot like dogs, especially German shepherds. But wolves have larger teeth and longer legs than dogs. They also have wider heads and longer noses.

Dogs use a similar body language as wolves. They give friendly licks. They wag their tails when they are being friendly or want to play. But there is a big difference. Unlike wild wolves, dogs are tame, or **domesticated**.

◀ Dogs like this German shepherd descended from wolves.

CHAPTER 5

# The Struggle for Survival

For centuries, many Native American people have seen wolves as **sacred** animals. But the early European settlers who came to America feared and hated wolves because they killed the setters' farm animals. Wolves slowly lost their habitat as settlers built farms and towns. They had less wilderness to roam and fewer animals to hunt. Nevertheless, farmers were allowed to hunt, trap, and poison wolves. Some states even paid people when they killed a wolf.

By the early 1970s, gray wolves had almost disappeared from the lower 48 United States. They had become **endangered** animals. In 1974, gray wolves were added to the endangered species list. It is against the law to hunt or capture animals on this list.

▶ **Wolves bare their teeth when they are angry.**

# A Return to Yellowstone

Yellowstone National Park is one of the oldest and most visited U.S. national parks. Located mostly in Wyoming, the park also spreads into Montana and Idaho. Many people go there to watch wildlife. There was a time when they would not have seen gray wolves, though. By the 1920s, all of the parks' wolves had been wiped out.

In 1995 and 1996, gray wolves were brought to Yellowstone from Canada. They quickly formed packs. The leaders had pups that later formed their own packs. Today, there are more than 100 wolves in the park.

Ranchers living nearby were concerned that the wolves would kill the animals they were raising. But scientists argued that the wolves benefited the entire ecosystem. Other animals eat food that wolves leave behind. Wolves also helped reduce the number of elk in the park. That is important because elk were eating too many aspen trees in the park. Without the trees, birds lost their homes and beavers were unable to build their dams. Without wolves, nature was unbalanced.

◀ Wolves in Yellowstone share their habitat with animals like this elk.

# The Future for Wolves

Thanks to conservation efforts like the one that brought gray wolves back to Yellowstone, these powerful predators have made a comeback in many parts of the United States. There are more than 5,700 gray wolves in the lower 48 states. There may be as many as 11,200 in Alaska. Canada has about 50,000 gray wolves.

Gray wolves have been removed from the endangered species lists in most states. In those places it is no longer illegal for ranchers to trap and kill wolves that they think are killing their animals. This makes conservationists worried. If wolf hunting isn't controlled, these amazing animals could once again be in trouble.

Some programs help release wolves back into the wild in places where they were close to disappearing. Wolves play a key role in keeping their natural areas healthy. Scientists hope people do their part to keep these extraordinary animals howling into the future.

▶ More than 65,000 gray wolves live in North America today.

# Gray Wolf Family Tree

Wolves are mammals that belong to the canine family. Like other mammals, they are warm-blooded, have hair or fur, and usually have babies that are born live. The diagram shows how wolves are related to other canines such as dogs, foxes, and coyotes. They all share a common canine ancestor that lived about 40 million years ago. The closer together two animals are on the tree, the closer their relation.

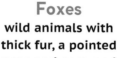

**Jackals**
medium-sized
wild dogs that
live in Africa
and Asia

**Foxes**
wild animals with
thick fur, a pointed
nose and ears, and
bushy tails

**Ancestor
of all
Canines**

*Note: Animal photos are not to scale.*

## Coyotes
animals that look
like small wolves and
live in the western
United States

## Wolves
the largest
members of the
canine family

## Domestic dogs
from poodles to
Labradors, there
are more than 300
breeds of these
popular pets

# Words to Know

**A** ............ **ancestors** *(ANN-sess-turs)* family members who lived long ago

**B** ............ **bonds** *(BAHNDZ)* close connections with or strong feelings for someone

**C** ............ **canine** *(KAY-nine)* one of the pointed teeth on each side of the upper and lower jaws

**D** ............ **den** *(DEN)* the home of a wild animal

**domesticated** *(duh-MESS-tih-kay-ted)* tamed in order to live with or be used by people

**dominant** *(DAH-muh-nuhnt)* most influential or powerful

**E** ............ **ecosystem** *(EE-koh-sis-tuhm)* all the living things in a place and their relation to their environment

**endangered** *(en-DAYN-juhrd)* a plant or animal that is in danger of becoming extinct, usually because of human activity

**endurance** *(en-DOOR-uhns)* the ability to do something difficult for a long time

**extinction** *(ik-STINGKT-shun)* the act of no longer being found alive

**G** ............ **glands** *(GLANDZ)* organs in the body that produce or release natural chemicals

**H** ............ **habitats** *(HAB-i-tats)* the places where an animal or plant is usually found

**herd** *(HURD)* a large group of animals

**L** ............ **litter** *(LIT-ur)* a group of animals born at the same time to one mother

**M** .......... **mammals** *(MAM-uhlz)* warm-blooded animals that have hair or fur and usually give birth to live babies; female mammals produce milk to feed their young

**mate** *(MATE)* to join together for breeding

**migrated** *(MYE-grated)* moved to another area or climate at a particular time of year

**N** .......... **nurse** *(NURS)* to drink milk from a breast

**P** .......... **pack** *(PAK)* a group of wolves

**predators** *(PRED-uh-tuhrs)* animals that live by hunting other animals for food

**prey** *(PRAY)* animals that are hunted by another animal for food

**R** .......... **rank** *(RANGK)* a position within a group

**regurgitate** *(ree-GUR-juh-tate)* to bring food that has been swallowed back from the stomach into the mouth

**S** .......... **sacred** *(SAY-krid)* holy, or having to do with religion

**species** *(SPEE-sheez)* one of the groups into which animals and plants are divided; members of the same species can mate and have offspring

**subspecies** *(sub-SPEE-sheez)* a group of related plants or animals that is smaller than a species; a division of a species

**T** .......... **territory** *(TER-i-tor-ee)* an area that an animal or a group of animals uses and defends

**tundra** *(TUHN-druh)* a cold, treeless area of far northern regions where the soil under the surface of the ground is permanently frozen

# Find Out More

## BOOKS

- Furstinger, Nancy. *On the Hunt With Gray Wolves*. Mankato, MN: The Child's World, 2016.
- Jazynka, Kitson. *Mission: Wolf Rescue*. Washington, D.C.: National Geographic Society, 2014.
- Llanas, Sheila Griffin. *Gray Wolves*. Minneapolis, MN: ABDO, 2013.

## WEB PAGES

- www.nywolf.org

  The Wolf Conservation Center provides up-to-date wolf news, amazing facts about wolves, and live videos from their wolf cams.

- www.nationalgeographic.com/animals/mammals/g/gray-wolf/

  Find fascinating facts and stunning photos at National Geographic's site.

- www.livingwithwolves.org

  This site is packed with information on wolves along with educational activities for kids. Find out more about wolf myths, learn how wolves communicate, and listen to wolves howl.

# Facts for Now

Visit this Scholastic Web site for more information on gray wolves:
**www.factsfornow.scholastic.com** Enter the keywords Gray Wolves

# Index

# Index (continued)

# About the Author

Lisa M. Herrington has written many books about animals for kids. While researching this book, Lisa visited the Wolf Conservation Center in South Salem, New York. She even got to howl with wolves there. Lisa lives in Connecticut with her husband, daughter, and three goldfish.